THE
ALASKA DISTILLERY
COOKBOOK
Inspired by Alaska Distillery Spirits

WITH
THE FLYING CHEF
MARK J. BLY

ISBN: 978-1-57833-972-3

Book Design: Vered R. Mares, Todd Communications

Published by
The Flying Chef LLC
A3-107 Arlon St.
Anchorage, AK 99507 U.S.A.
Tel. (888) 710-2204; Mark@TheFlyingChef.com
www.TheFlyingChef.com

Printed by Everbest Printing Co., Ltd., in Guangzhou, China, through **Alaska Print Brokers**, Anchorage, Alaska.

Distributed by
Todd Communications
611 E. 12th Ave., Suite 102
Anchorage, Alaska 99501
Phone: (907) 274-TODD (8633) • Fax: (907) 929-5550
email: sales@toddcom.com • WWW.ALASKABOOKSANDCALENDARS.COM

with other offices in Ketchikan, Juneau and Fairbanks, Alaska.

Alaska Distillery Cookbook Table of Contents

The Poultry

Sauces

Sweets

The Drinks

Foreword

Living in Alaska is as challenging as it is beautiful. Home to the tallest peak in North America, over three million lakes and over 100,000 glaciers! I feel very fortunate to live and work in a place of such grandeur.

After an aircraft accident, I hung up my spurs as a commercial pilot, and together with two friends and fellow pilots, started Alaska Distillery.

It's been a lot of hard work, but we have created some of the best spirits in the industry, partly due to the quality of ingredients that go into each bottle and partly due to our love of what we do.

Our distillery is located in the fertile Matanuska Valley at the foothills of the Alaska Range in South-central Alaska. We handcraft a variety of spirits using the highest quality ingredients and hand harvested glacier ice that we collect from free-floating icebergs from the Gulf of Alaska. No glacier is ever touched in our harvests.

We came up with the idea of a spirits-themed cookbook after some local restaurants started experimenting with our spirits in some of their dishes. We soon teamed up with Chef Mark Bly with the goal of creating a cookbook that was sure to please. After a year of hard work, we produced this very unique cookbook that we hope you will enjoy.

We appreciate your support and please drop us a line and let us know what you think of the recipes.

Cheers,

Toby Foster
Alaska Distillery

Dedication

Dedicated to the memory of my ever-present companion in the kitchen, Charles "Chuck" Wren Hoeck, my stellar Blonde Labrador who passed in January of 2013 after a noble battle with cancer.

Mark J. Bly
The Flying Chef

ALASKA DISTILLERY

Sides & Salads

FRENCH ONION SOUP

3 large onions, sliced thin
2 ounces clarified butter
3 quarts beef stock
4 ounces sherry
4 ounces Alaska Distillery Bristol Bay Gin
A sachet, or tea ball containing 3 parsley stems and 1 bay leaf
¼ teaspoon cracked black peppercorns
½ teaspoon thyme
Salt and pepper to taste
1 loaf dry French bread, sliced
½ pound Gruyére cheese

In a soup kettle or large soup pot, sauté the sliced onion in the butter until a deep brown color develops. Add small amounts of broth if necessary to prevent burning. If you are in a hurry, you can add a pinch of sugar at this point to speed caramelizing.

Add the sherry and deglaze. Continue to cook until the onions and broth are of a syrupy consistency.

Add the remaining broth and sachet of herbs.

Simmer for about 25 more minutes, and then remove the sachet. Add the Bristol Bay Gin and stir.

Salt and pepper to taste.

Serve in bowls and add some bread. Top with Gruyére cheese and place under a broiler until the desired cheese melt is achieved.

Serve carefully, because the bowls are hot!

MARINATED MUSHROOMS

1 pound small to medium-sized mushrooms, rinsed and trimmed
⅔ cup extra virgin olive oil
½ cup water
1 bay leaf
¼ cup Alaska Distillery Frostbite Vodka
Juice of 2 lemons
4 tablespoons red wine vinegar
4 cloves garlic, crushed
1 shallot, minced
6 peppercorns
1 red bell pepper, minced
½ teaspoon salt
¼ teaspoon basil
¼ teaspoon oregano
¼ teaspoon fresh minced rosemary
½ teaspoon red hot pepper flakes or to taste

In a large saucepan, add all ingredients except the mushrooms and bring to a boil over a medium-high heat. Reduce heat, cover and simmer for 15 minutes.

Remove garlic and peppercorns with a slotted spoon and return to a simmer.

Place mushrooms in simmering liquid and stir occasionally to ensure all pieces are basted for about 4 minutes. Depending on the mushroom size, it may take more or less time to accomplish.

Remove the pan from the heat and let cool.

When cool, serve or place in container in the refrigerator.

For best results, consume within 3 days.

MASHERS WITH BLUE CHEESE, BACON AND GIN

1½ pounds baby Yukon potatoes
4 slices bacon, cooked and crumbled
4 tablespoons butter
¾ cup Maytag Blue cheese
2 ounces Alaska Distillery Bristol Bay Gin
½ tablespoon Dijon mustard
1 teaspoon Worcestershire sauce
3 tablespoons chopped parsley
Salt and pepper to taste

In a large pot, boil the potatoes until done. Drain off the water and add all ingredients except the parsley. Mix ingredients and potatoes with a regular table knife until the desired texture is reached. Spoon into serving bowls and garnish with the parsley.

WHISKEY AND MOLASSES BAKED BEANS

4 strips bacon
1 large onion, chopped
1 green pepper, chopped
2 cans Rotel brand diced tomatoes with chilies
½ cup molasses
1 small can tomato paste
½ cup Alaska Distillery Whiskey
¼ cup brown sugar
2 tablespoons Dijon mustard
Salt and pepper to taste
1 can black beans
1 can white kidney beans
1 can red kidney beans

Cook the bacon until crisp in a large skillet. Set aside, cool and crumble. Pour off all but 2 tablespoons of the fat.

Add onion and green pepper to the skillet and sauté for about 8 minutes until soft and translucent.

Stir in the tomatoes, tomato paste, molasses, brown sugar, mustard, salt, pepper and Alaska Distillery Whiskey. Bring to a boil. Stir occasionally, and then simmer for about 3 minutes.

Add beans and crumbled bacon; mix.

Pour into a shallow baking dish and bake at 350 degrees in the oven for 45 minutes.

BLACKSTONE BAY SPINACH SALAD WITH A BIRCH FLAMBÉ

1 bunch fresh spinach, washed and dried
1 hard-boiled egg
A pinch of white pepper
A pinch of salt
4 strips bacon, fried and chopped
¼ cup bacon drippings
2 tablespoons malt vinegar
1 tablespoon lemon juice
1 teaspoon brown sugar
1 teaspoon Worcestershire sauce
1 ounce Alaska Distillery Birch Syrup Vodka

Tear your spinach and put in a large bowl. Slice the hard-boiled egg and add to the salad. Add salt and pepper.

In a saucepan, mix the bacon and drippings, malt vinegar, lemon juice and Worcestershire sauce. Heat until very hot, remove from heat and then add Birch syrup vodka. Ignite and when the flames go out pour over spinach. Toss gently and serve immediately.

Note: Be very careful when mixing grease and alcohol.

Keep all children at bay.

ALASKAN WHISKEY CHEESE BISCUITS

2 cups all-propose flour
2 teaspoons baking powder
¼ teaspoon baking soda
¼ teaspoon salt
1 teaspoon mustard powder
Cayenne pepper to taste
Black pepper to taste
½ cup heavy cream
½ cup buttermilk and a little bit extra for finishing
4 ounces cold butter, cubed
4 ounces Cambozola cheese
4 ounces sharp cheddar cheese
2 ounces Parmesan cheese
2 ounces Alaska Distillery Whiskey
Preheat your oven to 375 degrees.
Grate your cheese and set aside.

In a large bowl, thoroughly mix all of your dry ingredients. Next, rub in the butter with your fingers until the batter is the size of small peas. Add the cream, buttermilk and whiskey; mix gently with your hands.

Heavily flour a smooth work surface and place the ball of dough on top of it. Pat to a rectangle ½ inch thick. Place ¼ of your cheese on one side of the dough. Now, fold the dough over on itself and roll it out until it is again rectangular in shape and is ½ inch thick. Repeat this process until all of the cheese has been used. Cut your biscuits into the desired shape and quantity. You should be able to get 8 large biscuits or about 15 small biscuits out of the batch.

Place the biscuits on a greased cookie sheet and brush with some buttermilk and top with more black pepper.

Bake for about 7 minutes, and then turn the pan. Bake for another 7 minutes or until your biscuits are a golden brown.

Enjoy.

MINT AND CUCUMBER SALAD
WITH FIREWEED TAHINI VINAIGRETTE

Salad:

1 English cucumber, peeled, quartered, sliced
1 tablespoon fresh mint, chopped
1 tablespoon fresh parsley, chopped

Dressing:

2 ounces Alaska Distillery Fireweed Vodka
¾ cup extra virgin olive oil
¾ cup plain yogurt
2 tablespoons tahini
3 tablespoons fresh lemon juice
1 shallot, minced
1 clove garlic, minced
2 tablespoons agave nectar
¼ cup white wine vinegar
Sea salt
Cayenne pepper
Freshly ground white pepper to taste

Combine all dressing ingredients except mint and parsley in a blender and purée until smooth.

Add a pinch of cayenne or salt and pepper to taste.

Place the cucumber in a bowl and pour the dressing over it. Toss to coat. Place the salad on a plate and garnish with mint and parsley.

PURGATORY PESTO

1.5 ounces Alaska Distillery Purgatory Vodka
2 cups fresh basil leaves
2 large garlic cloves
¼ cup Parmesan cheese, freshly grated
2 tablespoons Pecorino Romano cheese, freshly grated
¼ cup pine nuts or walnuts
½ cup olive oil
Salt & freshly ground pepper

Combine the basil, garlic, cheeses and nuts in a food processor or blender. With the machine running add the Purgatory Vodka, then slowly add the olive oil. Season to taste with salt and freshly ground pepper and process to the desired consistency. Let stand 5 minutes before serving. Makes about 1 cup.

THE

ALASKA

DISTILLERY

Entrees

HONEY TERIYAKI FLANK STEAK

1 flank steak, 1 to 2 pounds
¼ cup Alaska Distillery Honey Flavored Vodka
¾ cup teriyaki marinade
2 green onions, chopped
1 tablespoon brown sugar
⅓ cup orange juice
2 cloves garlic, minced
Pepper to taste

Place the flank steak in a Ziploc bag. Mix all remaining ingredients in a bowl and season to taste, then pour them into the bag with the meat and marinate for a minimum of 1 hour.

When ready to grill, heat the gas grill to high—or for the purists out there—when your coals have reached their maximum potential, place the steak on grill and close the lid.

Cook for about 4 minutes per side and remove from the heat.

Let your meat rest for about 10 minutes.

Slice very thin against the grain and serve.

CARIBOU TAMALES WITH WHISKEY AND PEPPER

Filling:

1 pound ground caribou
2 Hatch chili peppers roasted and chopped
4 ounces Alaska Distillery Whiskey

Tamales:

2 cups masa harina
1 can beef broth
4 ounces Alaska Distillery Blueberry Flavored Vodka
1 teaspoon baking powder
½ teaspoon salt
⅓ cup lard
2 ounces Alaska Distillery Whiskey
1 package dried corn husks

Soak 12 to 14 corn husks in a bowl of warm water. This may take up to 3 hours. It may be necessary to weigh the husks down with a can or other object to keep them submerged.

Brown caribou over a medium heat. Drain off any grease. Add pepper and whiskey. Stir until the liquid is absorbed. Remove from the heat.

In a large bowl, beat the lard with a tablespoon of the broth until fluffy. Combine the masa harina, baking powder and salt; stir into the lard mixture, adding more broth as necessary to form a spongy dough. Next, add the remaining whiskey and blend into the mixture.

Remove the husks from the water and spread out on the counter.

Divide the masa mixture between the husks. Spread evenly and give yourself about a 2-inch margin from the edge of the husks.

Place a divided amount of the caribou and chilies atop your masa spread on the husks.

Fold the sides of the tamales first, and then the bottom up.

Place a steamer rack in the bottom of a soup-sized kettle and add water to the bottom of the steamer. Place the tamales vertically in the steamer and make sure your folds stay tight.

Place the lid on the steaming apparatus and steam the tamales on low to medium heat for 1 hour. Let cool and enjoy.

FILET MIGNON
WITH SWEET WHISKEY COFFEE SAUCE

2 or more tenderloins
¼ cup Alaska Distillery Whiskey
½ cup water
1½ teaspoons sugar
1 beef bouillon cube
½ teaspoon instant coffee or to taste
½ teaspoon ground pepper
¼ teaspoon salt
2 tablespoons butter

Place an appropriate-sized skillet on a burner and fire to a medium-high. Melt the butter in the skillet.

Season the filets and place in the skillet. Cook for about 3 minutes per side or until the desired done-ness is reached.

Let your meat rest.

In a saucepan combine the remaining ingredients over a medium heat, then reduce by two-thirds. Stir occasionally. Place filets on a plate and pour the sauce over the top.

If you like a thicker sauce, add some corn starch in the last several minutes of the boil.

GIN MARINATED LAMB CHOPS

6–8 lamb chops
2 tablespoons Alaska Distillery Bristol Bay Gin
2 tablespoons Worcestershire sauce
2 tablespoons lemon juice
2 tablespoons olive oil
2 tablespoons garlic powder
1 tablespoon seasoning salt

In a nonreactive bowl (nonmetal) mix all ingredients.

Place lamb chops in a large Ziploc bag and pour in the marinade. Seal and place in refrigerator for a minimum of 1 hour, although overnight is better.

When ready, fire up your grill and cook about 3 to 4 minutes per side over medium-high heat. When desired done-ness is reached, place on a plate and serve.

The result is a delicious lamb chop that is juicy and flavorful.

RING OF FIRE PULLED PORK SLIDERS

Note: This recipe will take two days or overnight to prepare.
1–4 pounds boneless pork butt
A few drops liquid smoke
Banana leaves
1 bag slider buns
Rub:
2 tablespoons paprika
2 tablespoons salt
2 tablespoons cayenne pepper
1 tablespoon black pepper
Sauce:
¼ cup Alaska Distillery Whiskey
1 can Embasa brand chipotle peppers in adobo sauce
¼ cup hot banana sauce
½ cup of your favorite BBQ sauce
2 teaspoons Worcestershire sauce

In a bowl combine ingredients for the rub.

Rinse off the pork butt and pat dry. Coat the pork with the rub and cover with plastic wrap. Refrigerate overnight or for up to 24 hours.

When rub marinating is complete plug in a Crock-Pot.

Line the bottom of the Crock-Pot with a banana leaf and place the pork in the cooker. Add a few drops of liquid smoke and cover the top of the pork with another banana leaf. Use more leaves if required. The key here is to tuck your pork in nicely so that the meat will baste itself.

Put the lid on your Crock-Pot and set the timer for 8 hours at a low heat.

When the pork is done the meat will no longer be pink. Most roasts these days come with a pop-up meat timer. Make sure that it has popped up and/or the meat is fully cooked.

Cool the pork butt, then pull apart or shred.

For the sauce, chop the can of chipotle peppers and place in a mixing bowl. Add the remaining sauce ingredients and mix.

Toast your buns slightly for that little "crunch."

Place your pork on the minibuns and spoon on the sauce.

Enjoy the heat.

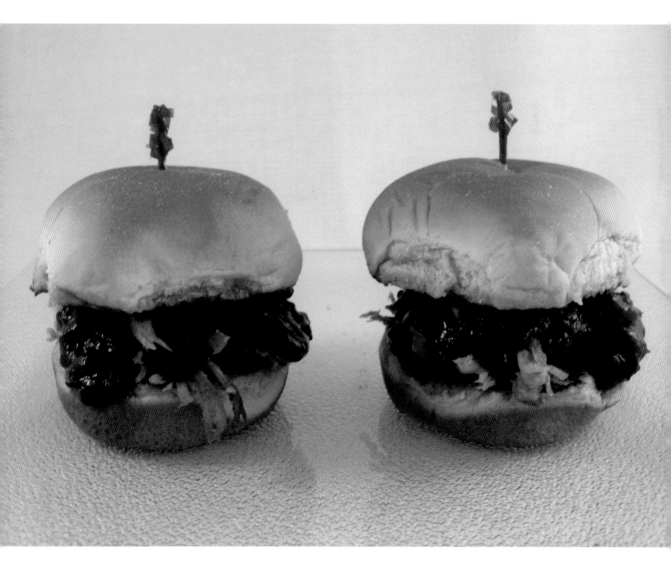

PORK LOIN IN A GIN AND ROSEMARY MARINADE

2 pounds fresh pork loin, trimmed and sliced
4 cloves garlic, chopped
5 capers, cut in half
1 tablespoon rosemary, finely chopped
1 tablespoon cilantro, chopped
2 tablespoons olive oil
3 tablespoons Alaska Distillery Gin
1 teaspoon sea salt
1 teaspoon pepper

Trim the pork loin and slice into approximately ½ inch medallions. Place the pork in a Ziploc bag or a nonmetal bowl. Mix the remaining ingredients with the pork and seal or cover. Marinate in the refrigerator for 30 minutes to an hour.

Heat a pan on a medium-high heat and add a ½ tablespoon of olive oil.

Remove the meat from the marinade and with tongs, carefully place it in the hot pan one piece at a time. I say carefully because the oil is hot and the gin used in the marinade will flare up as the alcohol burns off. Please be careful. Have a splatter guard or lid handy. A fire extinguisher is a good idea too.

Turn the pork when you just start to see the juices sweating out of the top. This will take about 2 to 3 minutes. Give it another 2 to 3 minutes or until the desired done-ness is achieved.

STEAK SINATRA WITH
ALASKAN BISON AND LINGUINE

2 pounds Alaskan bison tenderloin
4 tablespoons extra virgin olive oil
3 ounces Alaska Distillery Whiskey
½ cup red wine
1 onion, chopped
1 green pepper, chopped
8 or more artichoke hearts, chopped
10 plum tomatoes, halved
2 tablespoons fresh basil, chopped
10 or more pitted Kalamata olives, halved
6 baby portabella mushrooms, stemmed and chopped
4 cloves garlic, chopped
1 teaspoon dried oregano
Salt and black pepper to taste
One handful linguineParmesan cheese, freshly grated

This is a rich, decadent and hearty dish. All ingredients should be chopped into generous bite-sized chunks. Hey, this is about a legend, Frank Sinatra! Spare no expense and let the good times roll.

The idea here is to find the best quality meat you can purchase. Filet mignon works good too.

Start your linguine to boil in a large pot with plenty of water.

In a pan over high heat, add 2 tablespoons of the olive oil. Cook the bison for about 3 minutes per side, rare. Remove from the heat and set aside. Rest the meat at least 10 minutes, and then slice into bite-sized chunks.

In a deep skillet over medium-high heat, add the remaining 2 tablespoons of olive oil and add the garlic, onion and green pepper. Sauté until translucent, yet still a bit firm. Add the basil and mushrooms.

Now, pour in the wine and whiskey. This will deglaze the pan. Add the olives, tomatoes and artichokes. Stir in the oregano, salt and pepper to taste. I like lots of freshly ground pepper.

Add the meat. Simmer until the sauce thickens.

Do not overcook. If need be, add a tablespoon of corn starch dissolved in water to help speed things along.

Drain linguine and place on a plate. Ladle on the Steak Sinatra and top with freshly grated cheese.

ALASKAN CARIBOU POT STICKERS

½ pound ground caribou
¼ cup fresh Thai basil leaves, chopped
½ head cabbage, finely chopped
2 slices fresh ginger root, finely chopped
1 green onion, finely chopped
2 water chestnuts, finely chopped
Pinch of salt
½ teaspoon brown sugar
1 teaspoon sesame oil
5 tablespoons peanut oil
½ cup water
2 ounces Alaska Distillery Honey Vodka
1 package wonton wrappers

Sauce:
1 tablespoon chili paste with garlic
2 ounces Alaskan Distillery Honey Vodka
1 tablespoon soy sauce
1 tablespoon rice wine vinegar

Brown caribou in a skillet over medium-high heat. Stir in basil leaves until wilted.

In a large bowl, mix the caribou, cabbage, green onion, ginger, honey vodka, chestnuts, salt, sugar and sesame oil. Cover and refrigerate for a minimum of 4 hours, preferably overnight.

When ready to prepare, lay several wonton wrappers out on a clean surface. Have a small bowl of water to help seal the wrappers.

Place a tablespoon of your chilled caribou mixture on to the center of the wonton wrappers. Dip your index finger into the bowl of water and moisten the entire edge of each wrapper. Fold the edges on themselves and seal by pressing down with a fork. For a more unique look, seal the edges by pinching the edges of the wrappers.

In a large deep skillet, heat 3 tablespoons of peanut oil over a medium-high heat. Place your pot stickers in the hot oil, seam edges up. Heat for just under a minute and pour water into skillet. Gently boil for approximately 8 minutes until the oil and water begin to sizzle, then add the remaining oil. When the bottoms begin to brown, remove from the pan.

Sauce: Mix all ingredients and adjust to taste.

Dip and enjoy.

WHISKEY SHRIMP FLAMBÉ

1 pound shrimp, peeled and deveined
1 stick butter
¼ cup heavy cream
¼ cup Alaska Distillery Whiskey
1 tomato, diced
1 tablespoon lemon juice
Salt and pepper
½ cup Gruyére, shredded, and/or Parmesan cheese
¼ green onion, chopped

Melt butter in a large pan over a medium-high heat. When the butter is melted, add the shrimp and sauté for about a minute or until done.

Remove shrimp from the pan and set aside.

In the same pan add cream and tomatoes and simmer until thickened.

Turn the burner off and add the whiskey. Turn the burner back on and set the pan alight. Be careful, flames will result. This is normal. Have a lid standing by if things get out of hand.

When the flames die down, add the lemon juice and stir. Add cheese and melt. Return the shrimp to the pan and toss. When all is combined, serve.

LOBSTER IN WHISKEY CREAM SAUCE

2 lobster tails, cooked
1 stick butter
¼ cup Alaska Distillery Whiskey
¼ cup sherry
½ pint heavy whipping cream
2 green onion tops, diced
1 tablespoon minced garlic
½ cup Romano cheese, grated
¼ cup Panko bread crumbs
1 tablespoon brown sugar
Salt and pepper to taste
1 loaf French bread

Remove the cooked lobster meat from the shell and chop into bite-sized chunks. Sauté the green onions and garlic in the butter. Keep the heat low; do not scorch the butter.

Turn burner off, pour in the whiskey and light on fire. Be careful. Stand back and turn your vent on high. When the flame goes out, add the sherry. Next, add your cream and simmer on low until it thickens, about 15 minutes.

Add the brown sugar. Then add the lobster meat and heat. Keep stirring.

When the lobster is warmed through, remove from the heat.

Slice the loaf of French bread in half, then slice a small portion from the crust so it will rest evenly on the plate.

Place the lobster on a plate and sprinkle with the Panko bread crumbs.

Broil for a minute or two on at least the third rack down to avoid any burning. Keep a sharp eye on it. When you see the light golden brown appear on top, remove from the oven and serve.

EMPEROR'S HALIBUT

2 pounds fresh halibut filets
¼ cup Alaska Distillery Gin
2 tablespoons brown sugar
3–4 tablespoons black bean paste.
½ cup soy sauce
Small pinch of freshly ground ginger
4 green onions
Pepper to taste

In a nonreactive bowl, mix your gin, black beans, soy and ginger.

Add brown sugar to taste. You will see what I mean. The sugar will take the mixture from a tart salty taste to a well-rounded flavor. Use less sugar if you want a more Asian flavor or use more to mellow the taste.

Slice your onions into 3-inch pieces. Next, slice your onions lengthwise, and slice again. It should produce some nice green ribbons for garnish. If you want to get fancier, when slicing lengthwise, offset your knife about 30 degrees. It will produce an elegant tapered look. Just like the pros.

Slice the halibut into serving-size portions. Place the fish in a steamer and drizzle with the sauce. Don't be stingy; just be sure to save a tiny bit for serving. Toss on your onions and cook.

Cook in a bamboo steamer with a lid over a medium heat. It will be done when the fish flakes easily with a fork. Place a dash of gin in your steaming water for that "extra touch." If you do not have a bamboo steamer, try a vegetable steamer and a pan of water for steam. Heck, at camp, I even made this using a colander.

Enjoy.

EASY LOX

2 salmon fillets, bones removed
4 tablespoons coarse sea salt
3 tablespoons light brown sugar
1 tablespoon pepper
1 bunch fresh dill, chopped
½ cup Alaska Distillery Permafrost Vodka

Drape a plastic wrap over a glass baking dish. Place one fillet in the dish, skin side down. Mix together salt, brown sugar and pepper. Sprinkle half of mixture over the salmon in the dish, cover with the chopped dill, and pour the vodka over the whole mixture.

Sprinkle the remaining salt mixture over the remaining half of the salmon. Place over the salmon in the dish, skin-side up. Fold the plastic wrap snugly over the entire salmon. Place a board over the fish and weigh it down with a heavy object.

Refrigerate the fish for 24 to 36 hours, turning every 12 hours. To serve, separate the filets, and carefully brush off the salt, sugar and dill. Cut into very thin slices with a sharp knife.

Keep refrigerated.

FUN WITH SCALLOPS

2 pounds fresh Alaskan scallops
4 sprigs rosemary
3 tablespoons Herbes de Provence
1 lemon, sliced
1 package cedar wraps for smoking
Cooking twine
1 cup Alaska Distillery Whiskey

Place the desired number of cedar wraps in a shallow pan and add the whiskey. Allow it to soak for 30 minutes. Rinse your scallops in a bowl. Change the water often, and when the water remains clear, then drain the scallops.

Slice the lemon. Take a cedar wrap and place two scallops in the center. Sprinkle some Herbes de Provence on top. Add a slice of lemon and a twig of rosemary.

Tie the wrap closed on each end.

Cook using a low indirect heat on a grill. Indirect means that you heat only one side of the grill and put your wraps on the other "cool" side. Close the lid and cook for about 15 minutes. Remove from the grill, unwrap and enjoy.

SMOKED SALMON CHOWDER

1 pound smoked salmon
1 cup bacon, sliced
2 cups onion, diced
2 cups celery, diced
2 tablespoons garlic, sliced
2 cups potatoes, peeled and diced
1 stick butter
1 cup flour
1 quart milk
1 quart half and half
1 teaspoon thyme
1 teaspoon salt
1 teaspoon pepper
1 teaspoon nutmeg
1 teaspoon Worcestershire sauce
1 teaspoon Tabasco
1 quart chicken stock
3 ounces Alaska Distillery Smoked Salmon Vodka
1 ounce Marsala wine

Sauté bacon with butter 'til tender, then add onions, celery and garlic. Cook 'til onions are transparent or tender, then add flour and cook for 5 minutes. Add the potatoes and stock and simmer for 10 minutes, then add half and half and milk. Stir constantly so the flour doesn't lump up. Add the Smoked Salmon Vodka and add the Marsala wine. Simmer for 5 more minutes, then add smoked salmon. Season with Worcestershire sauce, Tabasco, nutmeg and salt and pepper.

HALIBUT CHEEKS

4 halibut cheeks or a nice filet cut in to 2-inch strips

Marinade:

3 ounces Alaska Distillery Purgatory Vodka
Juice of half a lemon
⅓ cup olive oil
Dash white pepper

Combine the vodka, lemon juice, olive oil and white pepper, then marinate the cheeks in the refrigerator for about 3 hours or until just before they start to turn translucent.

Soak an apple plank and when the cheeks are ready, place on the plank on a covered grill over an indirect heat, low to medium.

Check in 10 minutes and thereafter, every 10 minutes. You want the meat to start to flake with a fork.

Once cooked and full of smoky goodness, remove from the heat.

Sauce and pasta:

One handful or ½ box pasta
½ stick butter
2 tablespoons olive oil
2 ounces Purgatory Vodka or white wine
2 cloves garlic, minced
Handful capers

In a pot, boil your favorite pasta. Mine, in this recipe, is linguine. Al dente, of course.

In a small saucepan, add the butter, olive oil, the Purgatory Vodka or white wine, garlic and a handful of capers. Warm over a medium heat, just enough to evaporate some of the alcohol. Serve the halibut over pasta and add the sauce.

GOURMET SCRAMBLED EGGS
WITH ALASKAN KING CRAB

1 or 2 Alaskan king crab legs
8 eggs
2 tablespoons butter
1½ tablespoons sour cream
2 ounces Alaska Distillery Frostbite Vodka
1 green onion, chopped
1 teaspoon celery salt
Salt and white pepper to taste

Remove crab meat from the legs; pull into chunks or shred, then set aside.

In a large bowl, mix eggs, sour cream, vodka, green onions and celery salt. Add some white pepper and mix.

Heat a pan on a medium heat. Add butter and melt. When heated, pour in the eggs and scramble. Next, add the crab and cook to your desired firmness. Serve and enjoy.

CEDAR PLANK ALASKAN SALMON WITH MARTINI SAUCE

1 salmon filet
1 cedar plank
½ medium sized shallot, minced
2 tablespoons juniper berries, crushed
1 tablespoon green peppercorns, crushed
Juice of 2 limes
1 lime, sliced
3 tablespoons butter
2 tablespoons olive oil
1 tablespoon fresh parsley, chopped
1 cup dry vermouth
2 ounces Alaska Distillery Bristol Bay Gin
1 chive, chopped
2 cloves garlic, crushed
¼ cup green olives, sliced
Brown sugar to taste
Salt and pepper to taste
Cilantro, garnish

Soak a cedar plank in water for about an hour.

In a saucepan, combine vermouth, shallots, juniper and peppercorns. Bring to a boil and reduce by two-thirds. Add butter and stir until completely mixed. Remove from the heat.

Preheat your grill and place the sliced lime atop the cedar plank. Reheat the sauce and add the olives, gin, lime juice and garlic. Add salt and pepper to taste. If you don't like the flavor at this point, add a pinch or two of brown sugar. Carefully pour over the salmon filet. Use the sink so that the overage is an easy cleanup.

Sprinkle the filet with parsley and cilantro.

Place the salmon on the grill using indirect medium heat. Close the lid to cook.

Check on it in about 15 minutes. Salmon is perfectly done when you can see the fat just start to cook (the white stuff that starts coming out). If you're still not sure, take a taste and ensure the correct texture.

ALASKAN SMOKED SALMON EGG ROLLS

4 cups peanut oil for frying
3 ounces Alaska Distillery Smoked Salmon Vodka
3 eggs, beaten
1 egg white
½ head cabbage, thinly sliced
½ carrot, julienned
4 ounces shredded bamboo shoots
½ pound Chinese sausage, julienned
2 green onions, thinly sliced
2 teaspoons soy sauce
A pinch of sugar
A pinch of salt
3 slices fresh ginger, grated
½ Alaskan smoked salmon in small chunks
1 package egg roll wrappers

Put 1 tablespoon of vegetable oil in a large skillet or wok over a medium heat. Pour in the beaten eggs and cook without stirring until firm. Flip the eggs over and cook for an additional 20 seconds. The idea is make a pancake here. Remove from the heat and set aside until cool, and then cut into thin strips.

Heat the rest of the vegetable oil and add the cabbage, ginger and carrots. Cook until wilted, then add bamboo, green onions, salt, soy sauce and sugar. Pour in the Smoked Salmon Vodka. Cook until all ingredients are softened, add the egg and then remove from the heat. Spread out on a sheet or pan to cool. Refrigerate for at least 30 minutes.

Pour your egg white into a small bowl. On a clean surface, lay out a couple of egg roll wrappers at a time. Make sure one corner of the wrapper is facing you.

Spoon 3 tablespoons of the vegetable egg mixture on to each egg roll wrapper toward the bottom third of the wrap. Put some smoked salmon and sausage on top of the mixture. Brush some of the egg white on to the top edges of the wrapper.

Roll the wrapper firmly about halfway up. Now fold the left and right sides of the eggroll over the roll and continue firmly until the top corners of the roll meet the egg wash and seal.

Heat the peanut oil in a pan or wok. You are looking for a depth of about 6 inches for the oil. Your target temperature is 375 degrees.

Heat the rolls 3 or 4 at a time and blot on paper towels.

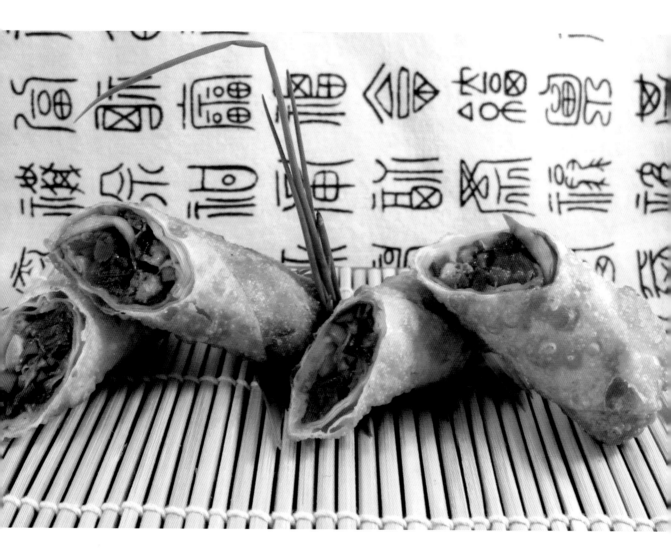

HALIBUT MARTINI EGG ROLLS

4 cups peanut oil for frying
1½ cups cooked shredded halibut
4 ounces Alaska Distillery Bristol Bay Gin
1 taro root
1 egg, beaten
1 egg white
½ head cabbage, thinly sliced
½ carrot, julienned
1 celery stalk, julienned
4 ounces shredded bamboo shoots
1 tablespoon fresh lime leaves, stemmed and minced
2 teaspoons soy sauce
A pinch of sugar
½ teaspoon celery salt
A small jar shredded pickled ginger
1 package egg roll wrappers

Peel the taro root. Boil for about 15 minutes or until soft. Drain and cool. Cut into chunks and add to the food processor. Mix until it turns into a paste. Add Bristol Bay Gin and mix until the liquid is absorbed. Cover and set aside.

In a large skillet or wok over medium heat add the tablespoon of vegetable oil. Stir-fry the cabbage, carrots, lime leaves and celery until wilted. Then add bamboo, salt, soy sauce, sugar and celery salt. Cook until all is softened, then add the egg and mix. Add the halibut and mix. Remove from the heat. Spread out on a sheet or pan to cool. Refrigerate for at least 30 minutes.

Pour the egg white into a small bowl. On a clean surface, lay out a couple of egg roll wrappers at a time. Make sure one corner of the wrapper is facing you.

Spoon 1 tablespoon of the taro gin mixture on to each egg roll wrapper toward the bottom third of the wrap. Spread 2 tablespoons of the halibut vegetable mixture over the taro paste. Top with the shredded pickled ginger. Brush egg white on to the top edges of the wrapper.

Roll the wrap firmly about halfway up. Fold the left and right sides of the egg roll over the roll and continue firmly until the top corners of the roll meet the egg wash and seal.

Heat the peanut oil in a pan or wok. You are looking for a depth of about 6 inches for the oil. Your target temperature is 375 degrees.

Heat the rolls 3 or 4 at a time and blot on paper towels.

THE FLYING CHEF WHITE TACO WITH HABANERO RASPBERRY PEACH HOT SAUCE

12 taco shells
¾ pound cooked Alaskan halibut, shredded or chunked
4 tomatoes, chopped
½ cup cilantro, chopped
3 cups cabbage, shredded
1 cup freshly grated Parmigiano-Reggiano cheese
1 cup Habanero Raspberry Peach* hot sauce
1 can black beans, drained and rinsed

OK, two schools of thought here. First off, I like to make my own shells, but, hey, this is your recipe, and if you lack the time or just prefer the convenience, by all means use store bought. Just try to purchase local if you can. Local anything is fresher by far. Have everyone assemble their own tacos, or you can do it all for them if you are so inclined. Heat your shells in the oven according to instructions on the box.

I prefer to spoon the black beans into the bottom of the shell. Next, add the halibut, followed by the tomato and cabbage. Pour on the hot sauce and trim with the cheese and sprinkle with cilantro.

Tacos are unique to everyone's taste, so experiment and enjoy.

*See page 90

SPICY ALASKAN FROSTBITE SHRIMP

1½ pounds large shrimp, cooked and peeled
1 red onion, thinly sliced
1 cup cilantro, finely chopped
1 cup lemon juice
¾ cup hot banana sauce
⅓ cup Alaska Distillery Frostbite Vodka
½ teaspoon Tabasco
¼ cup olive oil
4 Thai red chilies

In a bowl mix all ingredients except the shrimp and Thai chilies.

Depending on the amount of heat you desire, prepare the Thai chilies.

For low heat: add whole chilies to marinade.

Medium heat: slice Thai chilies and remove seeds.

Hot: slice Thai chilies and leave seeds in.

Figure out your heat index, then add chilies and shrimp to the mixture.

Cover and refrigerate for 6 hours. Drain and serve.

Serves 6.

ALASKAN LOCO CHICKEN

4 pounds chicken thighs, wings or legs
Marinade:
3 cloves garlic, minced
1 tablespoon white vinegar
½ teaspoon salt
½ teaspoon pepper
½ teaspoon dried oregano
½ teaspoon dried hot chili peppers, finely chopped
6 ounces pineapple juice
4 tablespoons lime juice
4 ounces Alaska Distillery Cranberry Flavored Vodka
A pinch of saffron (for color only)

Rinse the chicken and pat dry. Place in a Ziploc bag or in a covered glass bowl.

Mix all ingredients for the marinade. Using listed ingredients, you can adjust to fit your taste or just let it rip and pour it all into the bag with the chicken.

Refrigerate overnight, turning a few times to ensure proper marinating.

Place on grill over medium to low heat and cook until done.

GENERAL TSO'S BUZZED AGAIN LEMON CHICKEN

2 pounds chicken breasts, boned and skinned
3 cups peanut oil
1 cup Birds custard powder
3 tablespoons soy sauce
½ teaspoon sesame oil
2 lemons
2 garlic cloves
1 inch piece ginger
¼ cup chicken stock
¼ cup water
2 ounces Alaska Distillery Honey Vodka
1 teaspoon corn starch dissolved in water
1 teaspoon white pepper
White sesame seeds

Cut the chicken into 1 inch cubes and place in a mixing bowl. Add the soy sauce and sesame oil. Stir to coat. Cover the chicken and refrigerate for 30 minutes.

In a large bowl, combine the Bird's custard powder and the white pepper. Mix with a fork.

Drain the chicken and toss into the custard powder. Shake off any excess powder before frying.

Heat peanut oil in a wok or suitable pan until just smoking, and then turn down the heat slightly. Cook chicken for about 3 to 4 minutes or until done and it has a golden brown look. For best results, cook in batches. Drain on paper towels to remove any excess oil and set aside.

Remove the zest from one of the lemons. The zest is the yellow fragrant part. This can be done with a grater. Now cut the lemon in half and reserve the juice. Cut your other lemon into decorative slices and set aside.

Take 2 tablespoons of the peanut oil and place in a saucepan and heat to a medium high.

Mince your garlic and ginger, then cook until fragrant in the oil. This should take about 30 seconds. Add the lemon juice, zest, chicken stock, sugar and 2 ounces of Alaska Distillery Honey Vodka.

Reduce slightly, stirring all the while. Add the corn starch mixture to thicken and remove from the heat.

Toss the chicken in the sauce and put on a platter. Garnish with the lemon slices and white sesame seeds.

WHISKEY WINGS

1 bag frozen chicken wings
Sauce:
½ cup Alaska Distillery Whiskey
½ cup brown sugar
2 tablespoons white vinegar
2 tablespoons agave nectar
4 tablespoons butter
1 tablespoon garlic powder
1 tablespoon cayenne pepper or more to taste
2 tablespoons of your favorite hot sauce
2 teaspoons celery salt
1 tablespoon corn starch

Cook chicken wings in accordance with instructions on the package.

Mix remaining ingredients with the exception of the corn starch in a saucepan and place on a medium heat. Stir occasionally until the mixture begins to boil. Reduce the heat to low and simmer until the sauce reduces. This should take about 15 minutes.

Mix corn starch with a small amount of water, and then add to the sauce. Simmer for another 2 to 3 minutes, continuing to stir.

Remove from the heat and allow to cool. Toss cooked wings in the sauce and serve.

WHISKEY DRUMSTICKS

8–10 chicken drumsticks
3 tablespoons Dijon mustard
½ cup Alaska Distillery Whiskey
¼ cup agave nectar
1 tablespoon Worcestershire sauce
1 teaspoon paprika
1 teaspoon cayenne pepper
1 teaspoon onion powder
1 teaspoon garlic powder
½ teaspoon sea salt
½ teaspoon dried thyme
½ teaspoon dried oregano
½ teaspoon dried basil

Rinse and pat the chicken dry. Put into a bowl or Ziploc bag.

Place remaining ingredients in a blender and purée until well mixed.

Pour the liquid into the bag or bowl. If in a bowl, cover. If in a bag, seal.

Refrigerate and marinate at least 4 hours, preferably overnight.

Grill over indirect heat until reaching an internal temperature of 165 degrees and/or juices run clear.

THE
ALASKA
DISTILLERY

Sauces

RUSTIC ALASKAN VODKA SAUCE

Makes 3 cups (enough for 1 pound of pasta).

¼ cup extra virgin olive oil
2 ounces pancetta, diced
3 garlic cloves, peeled
¼ teaspoon red pepper, crushed
¼ cup Alaska Distillery Frostbite Vodka
1 tablespoon tomato paste
One 35-ounce can whole peeled Italian tomatoes with their juices, crushed by hand
Pinch of sugar
2 basil sprigs
¼ cup heavy cream
Salt and freshly ground pepper

In a large saucepan, heat the oil. Sauté the pancetta, garlic and crushed red pepper over moderate heat, stirring occasionally until golden, about 5 minutes. Deglaze with vodka. Add the tomato paste and cook, stirring for 1 minute. Add the canned tomatoes with their juices. Stir in the sugar and basil, season with salt and pepper and bring to a boil. Simmer the sauce over a low heat, stirring occasionally, until it thickens and is reduced to 3 cups, about 30 minutes. Season again with salt and pepper. Discard the basil sprigs and garlic. Add heavy cream and simmer for 5 minutes.

BASIC WHISKEY CREAM SAUCE

½ cup Alaska Distillery Whiskey
3 cups heavy cream
½ cup granulated sugar
¼ cup corn starch

In a medium-sized saucepan with the burner "off" pour in the whiskey. Add 2½ cups of the cream and the sugar. Turn on the burner to a medium to low heat and stir often to dissolve the sugar. Bring to a simmer and stir occasionally.

In a small bowl or measuring cup, add the remaining ½ cup of cream and stir in the corn starch. Add to the mixture and simmer for about 5 minutes or until the mixture begins to thicken.

Serve.

It can be stored for a day in the refrigerator in an airtight container. When ready to serve, warm it up slowly over a low heat.

ALASKA DISTILLERY WHISKEY BARBEQUE SAUCE

2 cups ketchup
¼ cup cider vinegar
½ cup yellow mustard
½ cup brown sugar
1 tablespoon onion powder
1 tablespoon chili powder
½ teaspoon red pepper flakes
2 tablespoons garlic powder
1 tablespoon freshly ground black pepper
½ teaspoon celery salt
½ teaspoon salt
1 tablespoon liquid smoke
3 tablespoons Worcestershire sauce
½ cup Alaskan Distillery Whiskey

Here's another easy recipe. Mix all ingredients in a saucepan and simmer over a low heat for about 25 minutes. Stir occasionally. Let cool and . . . yummy!

This sauce gets better when it sits awhile.

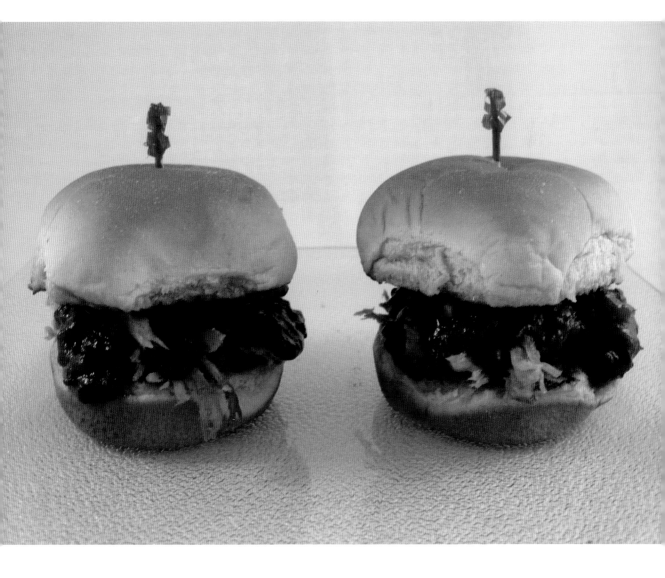

GOURMET HORSERADISH

4 tablespoons horseradish
1 jigger Alaska Distillery Gin
1 tablespoon fresh parsley, chopped
3 teaspoons sea salt
1 teaspoon fresh ground pepper

In a small bowl combine all ingredients except the gin. Then stirring with a fork, add small amounts of the gin until you achieve a desired consistency. It is better to be on the thicker side.

Cover, refrigerate and give it another stir just before serving.

HABANERO RASPBERRY PEACH SAUCE
TWO-DAY RECIPE

Day One:

6 ripe peaches
1 cup red wine vinegar
1 cup white wine vinegar
1 cup superfine sugar
3 ounces Alaska Distillery Raspberry Vodka
2 teaspoons sea salt
7 cloves
1 stick cinnamon
2 bay leaves
1 Mason jar

The peaches need to be "pickled" first.

Bring a large saucepan of water to a boil. Score the outside of the peaches and place them in the boiling water. Cook for about 2 minutes or until the skin begins to peel away from the fruit. Drain and cool.

When the fruit is cool enough to handle, peel the skin from the peaches, slice into wedges and place in the jar.

Combine the remaining ingredients in a saucepan and simmer, stirring occasionally until all solids are dissolved.

Pour into the jar with peaches and refrigerate overnight.

Serve with vanilla ice cream or save for the following recipe.

Day Two:

3–4 habanero peppers, chopped and seeded
2 ounces Alaska Distillery Raspberry Vodka
5 tablespoons white wine vinegar
1 cup chopped pickled peaches
½ cup chopped onion
3 cloves garlic, minced
2 tablespoons fresh lime juice
¾ cup fresh orange juice
A pinch of salt
4 tablespoons brown sugar
¼ cup chopped cilantro
2 teaspoons celery salt

Mix all ingredients in a blender. When thoroughly mixed, pour into a saucepan and bring to a boil over a medium heat.

Cool and serve.

Like it hotter? Leave the pepper seeds in.

Serve with white tacos.*

*See page 68

RASPBERRY VINAIGRETTE DRESSING

¼ cup olive oil
2 ounces Alaska Distillery Raspberry Vodka
¼ cup balsamic vinegar
½ cup white sugar
2 teaspoons Dijon mustard
¼ teaspoon dried oregano
½ teaspoon freshly ground black pepper, or to taste

In a blender, purée until mixed. If you don't have a blender, pour it in to a Mason jar, seal lid tightly and shake.

Promptly refrigerate unused portion. Hold for no more than 2 days in refrigerator.

FIREWEED VINAIGRETTE

2 ounces Alaska Distillery Fireweed Vodka
¾ cup extra virgin olive oil
¾ cup plain yogurt
2 tablespoons tahini
3 tablespoons fresh lemon juice
1 shallot, minced
1 clove garlic, minced
2 tablespoons agave nectar
¼ cup white wine vinegar
A pinch of sea salt
A pinch of cayenne pepper
Freshly ground white pepper to taste

Combine all dressing ingredients in a blender and purée until smooth.

Add more cayenne or salt and pepper to taste.

HONEY WASABI VINAIGRETTE

½ cup virgin olive oil
1 tablespoon soy sauce
¼ cup balsamic vinegar
2 ounces Alaska Distillery Honey Vodka
2 teaspoons wasabi paste
1 green onion, topped and chopped
1 teaspoon freshly grated ginger
1 teaspoon garlic powder
1 tablespoon agave nectar
1 teaspoon crushed red pepper flakes

Put all ingredients except the olive oil into a blender and purée. Gradually add the oil and blend until smooth.

Did it get too spicy? Add small amounts of brown sugar until the desired taste is reached.

Immediately refrigerate any unused portions and hold for no more than 2 days.

THE
ALASKA
DISTILLERY

Sweets

BLUEBERRY CHOCOLATE TAMALES

Filling:

1 pound blueberries
1 24-ounce package of semisweet chocolate chips

Tamale:

2 cups masa harina
1 can beef broth
4 ounces Alaska Distillery Blueberry Flavored Vodka
1 teaspoon baking powder
½ teaspoon salt
⅓ cup lard
1 package dried corn husks

Soak 12 to 14 corn husks in a bowl of warm water. This may take up to 3 hours. It may be necessary to weigh the husks down with a can or other object to keep them submerged.

In a large bowl, beat the lard with a tablespoon of the broth until fluffy. Combine the masa harina, baking powder and salt; stir into the lard mixture, adding more broth as necessary to form a spongy dough. Next, add the vodka and blend in to the mixture.

Remove husks from the water and spread out on the counter.

Divide the masa mixture between the husks. Spread evenly and give yourself about a 2-inch margin from the edge of the husks.

Place a divided amount of the blueberries and chocolate chips atop your masa spread on the husks.

Fold the sides of the tamales first, and then the bottom up.

Place a steamer rack in the bottom of a soup-sized kettle and add water to the bottom of the steamer. Place tamales vertically in the steamer and make sure your folds stay tight.

Place a lid on the steaming apparatus and steam the tamales on a low to medium heat for 1 hour.

Let cool and enjoy.

GOLDEN RAISIN HONEY DESSERT TOPPING

½ cup golden raisins
½ cup Alaska Distillery Honey Vodka

Put your raisins and honey vodka in a glass or plastic airtight container and refrigerate. For best results, let it sit for at least a day before consumption.

Use on ice cream or your favorite crème brûlée.

ALASKA DISTILLERY HONEY BUZZ CRÈME BRÛLÉE

8 egg yolks
2½ cups heavy cream
¼ cup superfine sugar
2 ounces Alaska Distillery Honey Vodka
6 tablespoons Golden Raisin Honey Dessert Topping (see recipe on page 98)
3 tablespoons confectioner's sugar

Preheat the oven to 350 degrees.

Pour cream and Honey Vodka into a saucepan.

Over a low heat, slowly bring to almost a boil.

Remove from the heat and let stand for 15 minutes.

In a bowl, mix the superfine sugar and the egg yolks.

Reheat the cream and gradually stir in the egg yolk-sugar mixture, stirring continuously.

When mixed, strain into 6 ramekins and place in a roasting pan.

Add warm water to the pan until it reaches halfway up the sides of the ramekins.

Place in the oven and bake for 20 to 25 minutes until the custard has set up.

When done, remove from the oven and allow the custard to cool in the pan with the water. When cool, refrigerate. Thirty minutes prior to serving, distribute the confectioner's sugar evenly on the tops of the custard.

Caramelize with a blowtorch. No blowtorch on hand? Place the ramekins in the oven 3 racks down from the top and broil. This will require your constant attention to avoid any burning.

Top with Golden Raisin Honey Dessert Topping and enjoy.

ALASKAN BLUEBERRY CRÈME BRÛLÉE

8 egg yolks
2½ cups heavy cream
¼ cup superfine sugar
2 ounces Alaska Distillery Blueberry Vodka
1 pint fresh blueberries
3 tablespoons confectioner's sugar

Preheat the oven to 350 degrees.

Pour cream and Blueberry Vodka into a saucepan.

Over a low heat, slowly almost bring to a boil.

Remove from the heat and let stand for 15 minutes.

In a bowl, mix the superfine sugar and the egg yolks.

Reheat the cream and gradually stir in the egg yolk-sugar mixture.

Be sure to stir continuously.

When mixed, strain into 6 ramekins and place in a roasting pan.

Add warm water to the pan until it reaches halfway up the sides of the ramekins.

Place in the oven and bake for 20 to 25 minutes until the custard has set up.

When done, remove from the oven and allow the custard to cool in the pan with the water. When cool, refrigerate. Thirty minutes prior to serving, distribute the confectioner's sugar evenly on the tops of the custard.

Caramelize with a blowtorch. No blowtorch on hand? Place the ramekins in the oven 3 racks down from the top and broil. This will require your constant attention to avoid any burning.

Top with fresh blueberries and enjoy.

ALASKAN RASPBERRY CRÈME BRÛLÉE

8 egg yolks
2½ cups heavy cream
¼ cup superfine sugar
2 ounces Alaska Distillery Raspberry Vodka
1 pint fresh raspberries
6 mint leaves
3 tablespoons confectioner's sugar

Preheat the oven to 350 degrees.

Pour cream and Raspberry Vodka into a saucepan and over a low heat, slowly almost bring to a boil.

Remove from the heat and let stand for 15 minutes.

In a bowl, mix the superfine sugar and the egg yolks.

Reheat the cream and gradually stir in the egg yolk-sugar mixture.

Be sure to stir continuously.

When mixed, strain into 6 ramekins and place in a roasting pan.

Add warm water to the pan until it reaches halfway up the sides of the ramekins.

Place in the oven and bake for 20 to 25 minutes until the custard has set up.

When done, remove from the oven and allow the custard to cool in the pan with the water. When cool, refrigerate. Thirty minutes prior to serving, distribute the confectioner's sugar evenly on the tops of the custard.

Caramelize with a blowtorch. No blowtorch on hand? Place the ramekins in the oven 3 racks down from the top and broil. This will require your constant attention to avoid any burning.

Top with fresh raspberries and mint.

Enjoy.

ALASKAN FIREWEED AND LAVENDER
CRÈME BRÛLÉE

8 egg yolks
2½ cups heavy cream
¼ cup superfine sugar
2 ounces Alaska Distillery Fireweed Vodka
10 fresh or dried lavender stems
3 tablespoons confectioner's sugar

Preheat the oven to 350 degrees.

Strip the lavender leaves off the stems and put them in a saucepan. Add cream and Fireweed Vodka to the pan and place over a low heat, then slowly almost bring to a boil.

Remove from the heat and let stand for 15 minutes. Strain out the leaves and pour back into the saucepan.

In a bowl, mix the superfine sugar and the egg yolks.

Reheat the cream and gradually stir in the egg yolk-sugar mixture.

Be sure to stir continuously.

When mixed, strain into 6 ramekins and place in a roasting pan.

Add warm water to the pan until it reaches halfway up the sides of the ramekins.

Place in the oven and bake for 20 to 25 minutes until the custard has set up.

When done, remove from the oven and allow the custard to cool in the pan with the water. When cool, refrigerate. Thirty minutes prior to serving, distribute the confectioner's sugar evenly on the tops of the custard.

Caramelize with a blowtorch. No blowtorch on hand? Place the ramekins in the oven 3 racks down from the top and broil. This will require your constant attention to avoid any burning.

Enjoy.

TRIPLE RASPBERRY CHEESE CAKE

Crust:

1¼ cups pecan shortbread cookie crumbs

2 tablespoons unsalted butter and a little extra for coating the pan, or take the easy route and just use a premade graham cracker crust

Filling:

2 pounds ricotta cheese
1 cup granulated sugar
⅓ cup all-purpose flour
1 ounce Alaska Distillery Raspberry Vodka
3 large eggs
2 egg yolks
2 teaspoons vanilla extract
2 teaspoons lemon zest
½ teaspoon salt

Topping:

½ cup raspberry jam
⅓ cup Alaska Distillery Raspberry Vodka
Several fresh mint leaves, chopped
1 pint fresh raspberries

Note: Ensure your butter, eggs, cheese and jam are at room temperature.

Crust:

Preheat the oven to 350 degrees and adjust a rack in the middle of the oven. Coat a 9-inch springform pan with butter.

Mix cookie crumbs and butter in a bowl.

Pour into your greased pan. Press crust evenly across the bottom of the pan.

Bake for about 15 minutes, or until you see a golden brown around the edges.

Cool on a wire rack.

Filling:

Put ricotta in a food processor; add raspberry vodka and blend until smooth. Add sugar and flour; pulse until mixed.

With the motor running, add the eggs and yolks one at a time until blended. Then add vanilla, lemon zest and salt. Do not overblend.

Pour the mixture into your pan with the crust and smooth the top.

Bake for 1 hour or until the cake is set and you have achieved a golden brown color.

Then remove from the oven and cool on a wire rack.

Topping:

In a saucepan over a medium heat add the jam and ⅓ cup Alaska Distillery Raspberry Vodka and bring to a boil. Reduce the heat and simmer to a reduction of half.

Remove from the heat and let cool for about 5 minutes.

To Finish:

Pour the topping over the cake. Distribute fresh raspberries over the top and sprinkle with chopped mint. Refrigerate and serve.

ALASKA DISTILLERY WHISKEY FUDGE BROWNIES

½ cup Alaska Distillery Whiskey
1⅓ cups sugar
¼ cup semisweet chocolate chips
1½ cups all-purpose flour
½ cup unsweetened cocoa
1 teaspoon baking powder
1 teaspoon salt
½ teaspoon vanilla extract
6 tablespoons butter
2 eggs

Top with Basic Whiskey Cream Sauce (see recipe on page 84).

Bring whiskey to a boil in a small saucepan. Reduce by half. Turn off the burner and carefully remove from the heat. This helps to avoid fires or flare-ups.

Add chocolate chips and stir until smooth.

Measure flour and level with a knife.

Next, in a large bowl, combine flour, cocoa, baking powder and salt. Blend with a fork or whisk.

Using a mixer, blend the sugar and butter. Add the remaining ingredients and mix until combined.

Spread your batter in a greased 9-inch square pan and bake at 300 degrees for 25 minutes, or until an inserted toothpick comes out clean. Cool pan on a wire rack.

FROZEN FRUIT WITH CHOCOLATE TREATS AND ICE CREAM WITH BIRCH SYRUP VODKA

4 ounces frozen berries. Blend and pour into a glass to be refrozen as a layer.

A large scoop of your favorite gourmet ice cream.

4 chunks of high quality dark chocolate for the top.

A dash of Alaska Distillery Birch Syrup Vodka

Thaw frozen berries just enough to slightly blend and pour into a glass. Refreeze.

Add the large scoop of ice cream, then place 4 or more chunks of dark chocolate on top and place back in the freezer until ready to eat.

When ready to serve, top with a dash of Birch Syrup Vodka.

Prep time: 10 minutes.

Serves 1.

SORBET

A few words about sorbet. All of the Alaska Distillery products, with the exception of the Smoked Salmon Vodka, make a delicious sorbet. Then again, maybe you will be the first person to invent smoked salmon ice cream. That would be cool!

Simply take your favorite fruit and chosen flavor of Alaska distillery and insert them into the recipe below. The sky is the limit. Have some fun and be good to yourself.

Enjoy.

2 cups fresh_____, frozen

2 ounces Alaska Distillery_____Vodka

2 tablespoons fresh lemon juice

¼ cup or more sugar

In a blender, place the frozen fruit, vodka and lemon juice. Blend well. Now add the sugar. Blend again. Taste. If needed, adjust with more sugar.

Once you have the desired flavor, transfer into a container and freeze. Taste again. If needed, add more sugar and blend. Refreeze.

When ready to serve, let it sit at room temperature for about 15 minutes to soften a bit, then serve.

This whole process, even if you need to refreeze, should only take about an hour.

STRAWBERRY RASPBERRY SORBET WITH HONEY

2 cups fresh strawberries, frozen
1 cup fresh raspberries, frozen
2 ounces Alaska Distillery Raspberry Vodka
2 ounces Alaska Distillery Honey Vodka
2 tablespoons fresh lemon juice
½ cup or more sugar

In a blender, place the frozen fruit, raspberry vodka, honey vodka and lemon juice. Blend well. Now add the sugar. Blend again. Taste. If needed, adjust with more sugar.

Once you have the desired flavor, transfer into a container and freeze. Taste again. If needed, add more sugar and blend. Refreeze.

When ready to serve, let it sit at room temperature for about 15 minutes to soften a bit and then serve.

This whole process, even if you need to refreeze, should only take an hour.

Introducing MAX, the Alaska Distillery Polar Bear!

And now
(finally),
THE

ALASKA

DISTILLERY

Drink
Recipes

Cabin Fever

2 ounces Alaska Distillery Rhubarb Vodka

1 ounce coconut cream

2 ounces pineapple juice, blended or mixed with crushed ice until smooth.

Garnish with a pineapple slice or a cherry.

Dirty Moose

2 parts Alaska Distillery Birch Syrup Vodka

1 part Kahlúa (or other coffee liqueur)

Serve on the rocks.

Frozen Tundra

2 ounces Alaska Distillery Cranberry Vodka

1 ounce Kahlúa

1 ounce cream soda

1 ounce orange juice

Midnight Sun

2 ounces Alaska Distillery Blueberry Vodka

1 ounce Blue Curaçao

1 ounce Grenadine

Squeeze of lemon juice

1 ounce orange juice

Alaskan Bloody Mariner

2 ounces Alaska Distillery Smoked Salmon Vodka

4 ounces Clamato juice

Squeeze of lemon juice

Dash of Worcestershire sauce

Dash of Tabasco

1 teaspoon of horseradish

Salt and pepper to taste

Garnish with celery and lemon wedge

Ice Fog Martini

1 ounce Alaska Distillery Gin

3 ounces White Crème De Menthe

Permanent Fund Martini

2 ounces Permafrost Alaska Vodka

1 ounce Triple sec

1 teaspoon Fresh lemon juice

1 dash orange bitters

Mosquito Mojito

2 ounces Permafrost Vodka

4 ounces Club soda

1 teaspoon Fresh lime juice

1 tablespoon Simple syrup

1 teaspoon Brown sugar

Juice of 1 large lime

Mint

3 Dog Night

3 parts Permafrost Vodka

3 parts Tequila

3 parts white rum

3 parts triple sec

3 parts gin

Lemon juice

Gomme Syrup

Dash of cola

Raspberry Cheechako-lat Martini

2 ounces Alaska Distillery Raspberry Vodka

1 ounce chocolate liqueur

Last Frontier Cosmopolitan

2 ounces Permafrost Alaska Distillery Vodka

1 ounce triple sec

1 ounce cranberry juice

1 teaspoon freshly squeezed lime juice

Garnish with lemon slice

Chocolate Raspberry Martini

1½ ounces Alaska Distillery Raspberry Vodka

1 ounce white creme de cacao

Chill vodka and creme de cacao. Pour into a chilled glass. Garnish with a chocolate kiss and a fresh raspberry.

Alaskan Chilly Pink Sunset

1½ ounces Alaska Distillery Raspberry Vodka

1 scoop raspberry sherbet

1 tablespoon frozen raspberries

Mix together in a blender with crushed ice until you reach the desired consistency. Serve in a hurricane glass with fresh raspberries.

Kodiak Island Raspberry Iced Tea

½ ounce Alaska Distillery Raspberry Vodka

½ ounce white tequila

½ ounce light rum

½ ounce raspberry liqueur

½ ounce gin

2 ounces cola

2 ounces sweet and sour mix

Shake all ingredients except the raspberry liqueur in a cocktail shaker with a bit of ice. Pour into a highball glass. Carefully layer the raspberry liqueur on top and garnish with a lemon wedge.

Raspberry Cosmopolitan

2 ounces Alaska Distillery Raspberry Vodka

⅔ ounce triple sec

1 ounce cranberry juice

½ ounce lime juice

Shake with ice, strain into a chilled cocktail glass and serve.

Raspberry Chi Chi

1¼ ounce Alaska Distillery Raspberry Vodka

12 ounces piña colada mix (preferably Bacardi)

1 scoop ice

¼ ounce puréed raspberries

Pour puréed raspberries into a glass. Blend 1¼ ounce raspberry vodka, 12 ounces piña colada mix and 1 scoop of ice until smooth. Pour over puréed raspberries in a glass. Serve with a straw and stir stick.

907 SinGin

7½ ounces Alaska Distillery Gin

1 12-ounce package lemonade mix

1 liter 7-Up soda

4–5 ice cubes

Lemon garnish

Put ice cubes or crushed ice in the bottom of a pitcher. Pour in a thawed 12-ounce package of frozen lemonade concentrate. Pour 4–5 shots of Alaska Distillery Gin (as much as you like for as strong as you like) into the pitcher. Fill up the rest of the pitcher with the 7-Up. Stir well to break up the frozen lemonade and chill in the refrigerator for 30 minutes. Garnish glasses or the pitcher with lemon. Serve and enjoy.

Gin and Pink

2 ounces Alaska Distillery Gin

5 ounces tonic water

2 dashes bitters

1 twist lemon peel

In a highball glass, almost filled with ice cubes, combine the gin, tonic water and bitters. Stir well and garnish with the lemon twist.

Cucumber-Rosemary Gin and Tonic

2 ounces Alaska Distillery Gin

5 ounces tonic water

3 cucumber slices

1 sprig rosemary

Juice of 1 lime wedge

Splash soda water

Place the cucumber slices at the bottom of the highball glass. Squeeze lime juice into a glass and slightly muddle the cucumber. Add a sprig of rosemary and fill the highball glass with ice. Add gin, tonic and finish off with a splash of soda water. If you prefer a less sweet cocktail, add less tonic water and more soda water. Enjoy!

Gin Daiquiri

1½ ounces Alaska Distillery Gin

½ ounce light rum

1 dash lime juice

1 twist lime

1 teaspoon sugar

Shake ingredients in a cocktail shaker with ice. Strain into an old-fashioned glass.

Garnish with a twist of lime.

Slippery Gin

1 teaspoon superfine sugar

1 ounce lemon juice

2 teaspoons water

2 ounces Alaska Distillery Gin

1 maraschino cherry

1 slice lemon

In a shaker half-filled with ice cubes, combine the sugar, lemon juice and water. Shake well. Strain into a highball glass almost filled with crushed ice. Add the gin. Stir well and garnish with the cherry and the lemon slice.

Charging Moose

1½ ounces Permafrost Vodka

½ ounce Campari bitters

½ ounce dry vermouth

Shake ingredients in a cocktail shaker with ice. Strain into a cocktail glass and garnish with a twist of lemon.

Mind Eraser

2 ounces Permafrost Vodka

2 ounces Kahlúa coffee liqueur

2 ounces tonic water

Pour vodka, Kahlúa and tonic water into an old-fashioned glass. Serve with a straw.

Frontiersman Birthday

¾ ounce Chambord Raspberry Liqueur

¼ ounce dark creme de cacao

1 ounce Alaska Distillery Birch Syrup Vodka

1 ounce milk

Add all ingredients in an ice-filled cocktail shaker, shake and pour into a martini glass.

Termination Dust

1 part Birch Vodka

1 part Kahlúa

1 part Baileys Irish Cream

1 splash Rumple Minze

1 part milk

Mix all ingredients in a shaker with ice, shake, then strain into a shot glass. The amount of milk is optional depending on desired potency of your shot.

Milky Way Martini

2 ounces Birch Vodka

2 ounces chocolate liqueur

1 ounce Irish cream

Combine all ingredients, mix, then serve without ice.

Dirty White Russian

2 ounces Birch Vodka

1 ounce Kahlúa

1 ounce light cream

Pour Birch Vodka and Kahlúa over ice. Top off with light cream and enjoy.

Frozen Honey Bee

4 ounces Alaska Distillery Honey Vodka

2 ounces Kahlúa

2 ounces cream (Baileys Irish)

2 ounces honey

5 scoops vanilla ice cream

Combine in a blender and blend until smooth. Enjoy with friends!

Snowed-in Cocktail

2 ounces Honey Vodka

2 ounces apple juice

2 ounces cranberry juice

½ ounce fresh lemon juice

4 slices ginger root (fresh)

1 teaspoon honey (clear)

Wedge apple (thin wedge to garnish, optional)

Shake with ice and serve in a highball glass.

Matanuska Hot Toddy (Polish Krupnik)

2 cups sugar

2 tablespoons cold water

4 cups boiling water

1 cinnamon stick

10 peppercorns

20 allspice berries

¼ vanilla bean (scraped and sliced)

¼ teaspoon nutmeg

2 cloves

1 orange rind

1½ cups honey

2 cups Honey Vodka

Heat sugar in 2 tablespoons of water until it dissolves, then stir in the boiling water. Add the vanilla bean, nutmeg, cloves, cinnamon stick, peppercorns and allspice berries. Bring to a boil, cover and simmer for 5 minutes. Strain the caramel mixture and return to the pan. Stir in honey and orange rind and heat, stirring until the honey has completely dissolved. Bring to a boil. Remove the pan from the heat and gradually stir in vodka. Serve hot or cold.

Lavender Rosemary Infusion

1 bottle Alaska Distillery Fireweed Vodka

1 sprig rosemary

2 sprigs lavender

Infusion jar with tight sealing lid

Rinse the herbs and place them a clean Mason jar or similar jar with a tight sealing lid.

Pour the vodka over the herbs and shake a few times.

Seal the lid tight and store the jar in a cool, dark place for 3–5 days.

Test the flavor of the infusion every day, beginning on the second day.

Once the lavender and rosemary flavor is to taste, strain the herbs from the vodka using a fine strainer or coffee filter.

Wash the jar and return the flavored vodka to it.

Store as you do other vodka.

Fireweed Nectar

2 ounces Fireweed Vodka

1 ounce Grand Marnier

1 ounce pomegranate juice

1 teaspoon honey

Combine, pour in to a glass of crushed ice and enjoy with a garnish of fresh Fireweed flowers.

Midnight Sun Millionaire

1 ounce Alaska Distillery Fireweed Vodka
4 ounces Perrier Jouët Fleur de Champagne
Fireweed flower for garnish

Pour the vodka into a champagne flute.
Fill with champagne.
Drop a single Fireweed sprig in the glass as a garnish.

Notes

Notes